Bold Moves

Bold Moves

Matthew Petchinsky

B old Moves: Building Courage to Live on Your Terms
By: Matthew Petchinsky

Introduction: The Pillars of Courage and Change

In a world often ruled by fear, conformity, and the quiet surrender of dreams, courage stands as the ultimate force that can break through the chains of limitation. It is the foundation upon which personal freedom is built, a prerequisite for living an authentic and meaningful life. Courage isn't merely the absence of fear; it is the willingness to act despite it. It is the bridge between who you are and who you have the potential to become.

This introduction serves as a guide to understanding why courage is essential for personal freedom and offers actionable insights into how you can create bold, transformative changes in your life. By embracing courage, you can unlock the doors to a future that aligns with your deepest values, aspirations, and truths.

Why Courage is the Foundation for Personal Freedom

Courage is the spark that ignites self-liberation. Without it, we remain prisoners of societal expectations, personal insecurities, and the fear of the unknown. Personal freedom—the ability to live life on your terms—requires breaking free from these barriers. Here's how courage forms the cornerstone of this freedom:

1. **The Courage to Face Fear**

   Fear is one of life's greatest inhibitors, whispering doubts into our minds and magnifying the risks of stepping into the unknown. Courage allows us to confront these fears, not by erasing them but by refusing to let them dictate our actions. It empowers us to take risks, knowing that growth often lies on the other side of uncertainty.

2. **The Courage to Be Authentic**

   Authenticity demands bravery. It requires shedding societal masks and embracing your true self, even when it means standing alone. Personal freedom is impossible without authenticity, as it liberates you from the expectations and judgments of others. Courage provides the strength to stay true to who you are, even when it's uncomfortable or unpopular.

3. **The Courage to Take Responsibility**

   Freedom is deeply intertwined with responsibility. It takes courage to acknowledge that you are the architect of your life, responsible for the decisions, actions, and outcomes that shape your journey. By owning your power, you reclaim control over your life and step into true freedom.

4. **The Courage to Persevere**

   Life's challenges can often feel insurmountable, and the road to personal freedom is rarely smooth. Courage is what keeps you moving forward, even when faced with setbacks, failures, and hardships. It is the resilience to rise again and continue pursuing the life you deserve.

How to Create Bold Changes in Your Life

Creating bold, transformative change requires a strategic blend of courage and action. While the path is unique for everyone, the following principles can guide you in making significant shifts:

1. **Define Your Vision**

   Change begins with clarity. Take time to reflect on what personal freedom looks like for you. Is it leaving a toxic job? Starting your own business? Strengthening your relationships? Write down your vision in vivid detail, as this will become your guiding star.

2. **Identify Limiting Beliefs**

   Often, the greatest barriers to change are the stories we tell ourselves—"I'm not good enough," "It's too late," or "What will people think?" Courage requires identifying these limiting beliefs and challenging their validity. Replace them with empowering affirmations that support your goals.

3. **Take Small, Consistent Steps**

   Bold change doesn't have to mean drastic, overnight transformations. In fact, the most sustainable changes often start with small, consistent actions. Commit to one courageous step each day, no matter how minor it seems. Over time, these steps compound into meaningful progress.

4. **Surround Yourself with Supportive People**

   Creating change is difficult when you're surrounded by negativity or doubt. Seek out people who inspire you, believe in your potential, and encourage your growth. A supportive community can provide the encouragement and accountability you need to stay the course.

5. **Embrace Discomfort**

   Growth and comfort cannot coexist. Every bold change will require stepping out of your comfort zone and embracing the discomfort of uncertainty. Courage is what allows you to sit with this discomfort, trusting that it is a necessary part of the transformation process.

6. **Celebrate Your Wins**

   Acknowledge and celebrate every victory, no matter how small. Recognizing your progress builds momentum and reinforces your belief in your ability to create change. Each win is a testament to your courage and commitment.

A New Chapter Awaits

As you embark on this journey, remember that courage is a muscle. The more you exercise it, the stronger it becomes. With each bold step you take, you'll find yourself shedding the constraints of fear and stepping into the expansive freedom of your true potential.

This book is your companion, filled with tools, strategies, and inspiration to help you cultivate courage and create lasting change. As you turn the page, take a deep breath and remind yourself: you are capable, you are brave, and you are ready to transform your life.

Chapter 1: The Anatomy of Courage

Courage is often romanticized as a trait possessed by heroes and extraordinary individuals, but in truth, it is a quality inherent in all of us. It may lie dormant, buried under layers of fear and self-doubt, but it can be cultivated and awakened. To fully understand courage and its transformative power, we must dissect its components, explore what makes people bold, and uncover how to overcome the fear and self-doubt that often stand in its way.

What Makes People Bold?

Boldness—the ability to take decisive action despite risks—is not a random trait bestowed upon a lucky few. It is the result of specific mindsets, habits, and emotional resilience. Here are the key elements that contribute to boldness:

1. A Clear Sense of Purpose

Bold individuals are driven by a clear sense of purpose. They have a strong understanding of what matters most to them and use this clarity as their compass. This purpose acts as a motivator, helping them navigate challenges and make decisions that align with their values.

- **Example**: A parent may find the courage to fight for their child's education, not because they are fearless, but because their love and purpose overshadow their fear.

2. Resilience to Failure

Bold people view failure not as a permanent state but as a stepping stone to success. They reframe setbacks as learning opportunities, allowing them to take risks without being paralyzed by the fear of making mistakes.

- **Key Mindset**: "Every failure teaches me something valuable."

3. Emotional Regulation

Courageous individuals don't ignore their fear; they manage it. By understanding their emotions and employing techniques like mindfulness, deep breathing, or visualization, they can stay calm and focused even in high-pressure situations.

4. Self-Belief

Boldness stems from a deep-seated belief in one's ability to overcome obstacles. This confidence is not necessarily innate but is often built through practice, preparation, and small wins.

- **Practical Tip**: Regularly reflect on past successes to remind yourself of your capability.

5. Willingness to Take Calculated Risks

Boldness does not mean recklessness. Courageous people assess risks thoughtfully and are willing to move forward when the potential rewards outweigh the dangers. They understand that some degree of uncertainty is inevitable but not insurmountable.

Overcoming Fear and Self-Doubt

Fear and self-doubt are the two greatest adversaries of courage. They create mental barriers that prevent us from stepping into our potential. To cultivate boldness, we must confront and neutralize these forces.

Understanding Fear

Fear is a natural response designed to protect us from danger. However, in modern life, fear often manifests as an exaggerated reaction to perceived threats—like failure, rejection, or judgment—that are rarely life-threatening.

1. **Recognize the Fear**
   - Identify the root of your fear. Is it fear of failure? Fear of the unknown? Fear of being judged? Naming your fear is the first step toward overcoming it.

2. **Reframe the Threat**
   - Ask yourself, "What's the worst that could happen?" and then counter it with, "What's the best that could happen?" This shift in perspective helps you focus on the potential rewards instead of the risks.

3. **Practice Exposure**
   - Gradually expose yourself to situations that trigger fear. Each small victory builds your confidence and reduces the intensity of the fear over time.

Addressing Self-Doubt

Self-doubt is the inner critic that questions your worth, capabilities, and decisions. Left unchecked, it can be paralyzing. However, there are strategies to silence this voice:

1. **Challenge Negative Beliefs**
   - Write down the self-doubts that plague you and then counter each one with evidence to the contrary. For example:
     - Doubt: "I'm not smart enough to succeed."
     - Counter: "I've successfully learned new skills before, and I can do it again."
2. **Focus on Growth, Not Perfection**
   - Shift your mindset from "I need to get it right" to "I need to keep learning." This reduces the pressure to be flawless and encourages you to take action.
3. **Surround Yourself with Positivity**
   - Seek out people who uplift and encourage you. Avoid environments or individuals that amplify your self-doubt.

Action Steps to Build Courage

To strengthen your boldness and overcome fear and self-doubt, incorporate these practical exercises into your daily life:

1. **Visualization Practice**
   - Spend five minutes each day visualizing yourself succeeding in a situation that currently feels intimidating. Picture every detail—your actions, the outcome, and your sense of accomplishment.

2. **The "Courage Journal"**
   - At the end of each day, write down one courageous act you performed, no matter how small. Over time, this journal will serve as a powerful reminder of your growing boldness.

3. **Take Daily Risks**
   - Commit to one small, uncomfortable action each day. This could be starting a conversation with a stranger, voicing your opinion in a meeting, or trying something new. These micro-risks build your courage muscle.

4. **Affirmations for Courage**
   - Create a list of affirmations that resonate with you, such as:
     - "I am stronger than my fears."
     - "I have the power to face any challenge."
     - "Courage grows with every step I take."
   - Repeat these affirmations each morning to set a confident tone for the day.

The Anatomy of Courage in Action

Imagine a young entrepreneur who has a groundbreaking idea but is terrified of failure. By understanding the anatomy of courage, they learn to recognize their fear of rejection, reframe it as an opportunity for growth, and take calculated risks to bring their vision to life. Each step forward builds their self-belief, and over time, they transform from someone hesitant and unsure into a bold, confident leader.

This transformation is possible for anyone. Courage is not a fixed trait but a skill that grows with practice. By understanding what makes people bold and actively working to overcome fear and self-doubt, you can cultivate the courage necessary to create a life of authenticity, purpose, and freedom.

Chapter 2: Starting Small, Dreaming Big

In the journey toward personal freedom and achieving your dreams, it's tempting to believe that courage is only meaningful when expressed in grand, life-altering acts. However, this couldn't be further from the truth. Courage often begins with small, seemingly insignificant actions that, when repeated and compounded, lead to massive growth and transformation. This chapter delves into the power of small acts of courage, illustrating how they can snowball into significant life changes. We'll also explore inspiring stories of people who started small but dared to dream big, proving that every great achievement begins with a single step.

How Small Acts of Courage Lead to Massive Growth

Small acts of courage are the foundation of lasting change. While they may not seem groundbreaking in the moment, these actions create momentum, build confidence, and ultimately pave the way for monumental achievements. Here's how:

1. Building the Courage Muscle

- Courage, much like a muscle, strengthens with use. Each time you perform a small act of bravery—whether it's speaking up in a meeting, trying something new, or setting a boundary—you reinforce your ability to act despite fear. Over time, this practice makes facing larger challenges more manageable.
- **Example**: Imagine someone who fears public speaking. Their first act of courage might be raising their hand in a small group discussion. Over time, this confidence grows, and they eventually feel prepared to present in front of a larger audience.

2. Creating Momentum

- Small courageous actions create a ripple effect. Each success builds momentum, making the next challenge feel less daunting. This process transforms courage into a habit, propelling you toward bigger goals.
- **Key Insight**: "The journey of a thousand miles begins with a single step." Each small step reduces the mental barrier to taking the next one.

3. Shifting Limiting Beliefs

- By taking small actions, you challenge and reframe limiting beliefs about what you're capable of. Each small success becomes evidence that you are stronger, smarter, and braver than you initially thought.
- **Reflection Question**: What small courageous act can you take today that contradicts a negative belief you hold about yourself?

4. Unlocking Opportunities

- Small acts of courage often lead to unexpected opportunities. Saying "yes" to a new experience or reaching out to someone for advice can open doors you never imagined. These small moments are often the catalysts for significant life changes.

Stories of People Who Started Small

History is filled with examples of individuals who achieved greatness by starting with small acts of courage. Their stories demonstrate that no dream is too big if you are willing to take small, consistent steps toward it.

1. J.K. Rowling: A Single Idea, a Global Phenomenon

- **The Beginning**: Before she became the author of the *Harry Potter* series, J.K. Rowling was a single mother struggling to make ends meet. Her courageous decision to begin writing her story on scraps of paper in cafes was a small but bold act of defiance against her circumstances.
- **The Growth**: Rejected by multiple publishers, Rowling persisted, submitting her manuscript again and again. Her courage to keep trying led to one of the most successful literary franchises in history.
- **Takeaway**: Every big dream starts small. Rowling's courage to write her story one page at a time, despite uncertainty, exemplifies the power of small actions.

2. Mahatma Gandhi: The Power of a Simple Protest

- **The Beginning**: Gandhi's first act of courage wasn't leading a massive movement; it was refusing to move to the back of a train in South Africa because of his race. This small act of resistance set the stage for a lifetime of activism.
- **The Growth**: Over time, Gandhi's courage inspired millions to adopt nonviolent resistance, leading to India's independence from British rule.

- **Takeaway**: A single act of courage can ignite a movement. Gandhi's decision to stand up for himself in a small moment created a ripple effect that changed the course of history.

3. Oprah Winfrey: From Local News Anchor to Global Icon

- **The Beginning**: Oprah Winfrey's first steps toward success were small. She began as a news anchor at a local television station, often facing criticism and challenges because of her unconventional style.
- **The Growth**: Through consistent hard work and the courage to be authentic, she transformed her local presence into a global platform, becoming one of the most influential women in the world.
- **Takeaway**: Starting small doesn't mean staying small. Oprah's courage to embrace her uniqueness allowed her to grow beyond what anyone thought possible.

Practical Steps to Start Small and Dream Big

Starting small doesn't mean settling for mediocrity—it's about creating a foundation for exponential growth. Here are actionable steps to begin your journey:

1. Set Micro-Goals

- Break down your big dreams into small, manageable steps. Instead of focusing on the daunting end goal, identify the first actionable step you can take today.
- **Example**: If your dream is to write a book, start by committing to writing 200 words a day.

2. Celebrate Small Wins

- Acknowledge and celebrate every step forward, no matter how small. This builds positive reinforcement and motivates you to keep going.
- **Reflection Prompt**: What small win did you achieve today, and how can you celebrate it?

3. Embrace Consistency Over Perfection

- Consistency is more important than perfection. Focus on showing up daily, even if your efforts aren't flawless. Over time, your consistency will lead to mastery.
- **Practical Tip**: Use a habit tracker to monitor your daily progress toward your goals.

4. Seek Inspiration from Others

- Read stories, watch interviews, or follow individuals who started small and achieved big dreams. Their journeys will remind you that success is a process, not an overnight event.

5. Take Small Risks Daily

- Make it a habit to step out of your comfort zone in small ways. These daily acts of courage build resilience and prepare you for bigger challenges.
- **Challenge**: Identify one thing that scares you slightly and commit to doing it today.

The Big Picture: Small Acts, Big Dreams

Small acts of courage are the seeds from which massive growth emerges. They may feel insignificant in the moment, but their cumulative effect is transformative. When you dream big but start small, you create a roadmap to success that is both achievable and inspiring.

As you reflect on this chapter, consider the power of the small steps you can take today. No matter how big your dreams are, the journey always begins with a single act of courage. Take that step, and watch as your small beginnings evolve into something extraordinary.

Chapter 3: Facing Your Fears Head-On

Fear is a natural part of the human experience. It's our brain's way of protecting us from harm, but in today's world, it often acts as a barrier rather than a shield. Fear can paralyze us, keeping us from pursuing dreams, building meaningful relationships, or making life-altering decisions. However, the antidote to fear isn't avoidance—it's confrontation. This chapter explores practical steps to face your fears head-on and turn setbacks into stepping stones for growth and resilience.

Practical Steps to Confront Fears

Confronting fear doesn't mean eliminating it entirely. Fear will always exist, but you can learn to manage it and act in spite of it. Here are actionable steps to face your fears directly:

1. Name Your Fear

- Begin by identifying and articulating your fear. Often, fear feels overwhelming because it is vague or undefined. Giving it a name helps you understand and begin to address it.
- **Exercise**: Write down the specific fear holding you back. For example:
    - "I'm afraid of failing at my new business venture."
    - "I'm scared of public speaking because I fear embarrassment."

2. Understand the Root Cause

- Ask yourself: Where is this fear coming from? Is it based on a past experience, societal expectations, or self-doubt? Understanding the source of your fear can make it feel less daunting.
- **Reflection Prompt**: "What event or belief triggered this fear?"

3. Break Fear into Manageable Parts

- Fear often feels insurmountable because we view it as one large, unmanageable entity. Break it down into smaller, actionable components. For instance:
    - Fear: "I'm scared of public speaking."
    - Actionable Steps: Practice speaking in front of a mirror, then in front of a trusted friend, and gradually increase your audience.

4. Create a Fear Hierarchy

- Rank your fears from least to most intimidating. Start by addressing the smallest fear first, gradually working your way up the hierarchy.
- **Example**: If you fear rejection, begin by initiating small conversations with strangers before tackling larger challenges like asking for a promotion.

5. Use Visualization Techniques

- Visualize yourself successfully confronting and overcoming your fear. Picture the process in detail—how you feel, what actions you take, and the positive outcome.
- **Guided Visualization**: Close your eyes and imagine stepping onto a stage, speaking confidently, and receiving applause. This mental rehearsal can make the real experience less intimidating.

6. Take Incremental Action

- Start small and build momentum. Each step you take reinforces your courage and weakens the grip of fear.
- **Example**: If you're afraid of networking, commit to attending one event and introducing yourself to one person. Celebrate that win before moving on to bigger goals.

7. Reframe Fear as Growth

- Shift your perspective to see fear as an opportunity for growth. Instead of thinking, "What if I fail?" ask, "What will I learn?"
- **Mantra**: "Fear is a signal that I'm stepping out of my comfort zone and growing."

8. Seek Support and Accountability

- Share your fears with trusted friends, mentors, or a support group. They can offer encouragement, perspective, and accountability as you face your challenges.
- **Tip**: Find someone who has overcome a similar fear and learn from their journey.

9. Practice Mindfulness and Relaxation

- Fear often triggers physical responses like a racing heart or shallow breathing. Mindfulness practices such as deep breathing, meditation, or yoga can help you stay calm and present.

- **Quick Exercise**: Inhale deeply for four counts, hold for four counts, and exhale for six counts. Repeat until you feel more centered.

10. Celebrate Every Victory

- Acknowledge and reward yourself for every step you take toward facing your fear. These victories, no matter how small, build confidence and reinforce your courage.

Turning Setbacks into Stepping Stones

Setbacks are inevitable, especially when confronting fear. What matters is how you respond to them. By reframing setbacks as opportunities for growth, you can turn even the most challenging moments into valuable lessons.

1. Embrace Failure as a Teacher

- Failure isn't the opposite of success—it's a critical part of it. Every setback offers insights that can help you refine your approach and improve.
- **Reflection Prompt**: "What can I learn from this experience, and how can I apply it moving forward?"

2. Reframe the Narrative

- Instead of viewing setbacks as proof of inadequacy, see them as milestones on your journey. Each setback is evidence that you're trying, learning, and progressing.
- **Example**: If you bomb a presentation, remind yourself that even seasoned speakers have off days. Focus on what you did well and what you can improve.

3. Build Resilience Through Reflection

- After a setback, take time to reflect on what went wrong and why. This analysis helps you make more informed decisions in the future.
- **Journal Exercise**: Write down the event, what you felt, what you learned, and what you'll do differently next time.

4. Stay Focused on the Big Picture

- Setbacks can feel overwhelming in the moment, but they are just one part of a larger journey. Keep your long-term goals in mind to maintain perspective.
- **Visualization Tip**: Create a vision board or write a mission statement to remind yourself of your ultimate purpose.

5. Lean on Your Support Network

- Share your setbacks with others who can offer encouragement, advice, and perspective. A strong support network helps you bounce back more quickly.
- **Tip**: Join a community of like-minded individuals who understand your struggles and celebrate your progress.

6. Keep Taking Action

- The best way to recover from a setback is to keep moving forward. Even a small action can reignite your momentum and rebuild your confidence.
- **Challenge**: After experiencing a setback, identify one immediate step you can take to get back on track.

7. Celebrate Progress, Not Perfection

- Progress is rarely linear. Celebrate the fact that you're making the effort, even if the journey includes detours and delays.
- **Mantra**: "Every step forward, no matter how small, is a victory."

Real-Life Examples of Overcoming Fear and Setbacks
1. Thomas Edison: Persistence Through Setbacks

- Edison famously said, "I have not failed. I've just found 10,000 ways that won't work." His willingness to view each setback as a learning opportunity led to the invention of the light bulb.
- **Takeaway**: Reframe failure as data. Each setback is a step closer to success.

2. Serena Williams: Conquering Pressure and Setbacks

- Serena Williams, one of the greatest athletes in history, has faced injuries, personal challenges, and public scrutiny. Her resilience and ability to confront fear head-on have allowed her to maintain her dominance in tennis.
- **Takeaway**: Resilience comes from confronting challenges with determination and learning from each experience.

3. Walt Disney: Rejection as a Stepping Stone

- Early in his career, Walt Disney was fired from a newspaper for "lacking imagination." Instead of giving up, he used this setback as motivation to create what would become one of the most imaginative and successful companies in the world.
- **Takeaway**: Rejection is not the end of the road; it's a redirection toward something better.

Facing Your Fears: A New Chapter

Facing your fears head-on is a transformative process that empowers you to live boldly and authentically. By taking small, actionable steps and reframing setbacks as stepping stones, you can build the courage and resilience needed to overcome any challenge.

As you move forward, remember that fear is not your enemy—it's a sign that you're stepping into uncharted territory and growing. Embrace it, confront it, and let it propel you toward your goals.

Chapter 4: Taking Risks with Confidence

Life is inherently risky. Whether it's pursuing a career change, starting a new relationship, or making a significant financial investment, risk is an inescapable part of growth and achievement. However, not all risks are created equal. Some are reckless leaps in the dark, while others are calculated steps forward with a foundation of thought and preparation. Taking risks with confidence requires striking a balance between rational decision-making and trusting your intuition. This chapter explores how to calculate risks intelligently while harnessing the power of your gut instinct in bold moments.

Calculating Risks for Smart Decision-Making

Taking risks does not mean acting impulsively or without consideration. Smart decision-making is about assessing the potential outcomes and making informed choices that align with your goals. Here's how to approach risk-taking with a calculated mindset:

1. Clearly Define Your Goal

- Before taking any risk, identify what you hope to achieve. A clear goal provides focus and ensures that the risk aligns with your long-term objectives.
- **Exercise**: Write down your desired outcome. Ask yourself, "What do I stand to gain if this risk succeeds?"

2. Evaluate the Potential Rewards

- Assess the upside of taking the risk. What are the tangible and intangible benefits if everything goes as planned? Understanding the rewards helps you stay motivated and focused.

- **Example**: If you're considering starting a business, the rewards might include financial independence, creative freedom, and personal fulfillment.

3. Assess the Potential Downsides

- Consider the worst-case scenario. What could go wrong, and how would you handle it? Preparing for possible setbacks helps you mitigate their impact and reduces fear of the unknown.
- **Exercise**: List the risks involved and brainstorm solutions for each. For example:
    - Risk: Losing money.
    - Mitigation: Start with a smaller investment or secure a backup income source.

4. Weigh the Odds

- Determine the likelihood of success versus failure. While no risk is guaranteed, understanding the probability of different outcomes can guide your decision-making.
- **Practical Tip**: Research similar scenarios or seek advice from people who have taken similar risks to gauge potential outcomes.

5. Conduct a Risk-Reward Analysis

- Compare the potential rewards to the potential costs. Ask yourself:
    - Is the reward worth the risk?
    - Can I accept the consequences if things don't go as planned?

6. Start Small and Scale Up

- If possible, test your risk on a smaller scale before committing fully. This approach allows you to gather data and adjust your strategy while minimizing potential losses.
- **Example**: Before launching a full business, test your product or service with a small audience to gauge interest.

7. Create a Contingency Plan

- Have a backup plan in place. Knowing you have a safety net reduces anxiety and gives you the confidence to move forward.
- **Practical Tip**: Outline steps you can take to recover if the risk doesn't pay off.

8. Commit Once Decided

- Once you've calculated the risk and decided to move forward, commit fully. Indecision and hesitation can undermine your efforts and increase the likelihood of failure.

Trusting Your Intuition in Bold Moments

While logic and analysis are essential for smart decision-making, intuition often plays a critical role in moments of bold action. Intuition—our gut feeling—is the result of subconscious processing based on past experiences, knowledge, and emotions. Here's how to harness your intuition effectively:

1. Understand the Role of Intuition

- Intuition isn't magical; it's your brain's way of synthesizing information quickly and presenting it as a feeling or hunch. Trusting your intuition means learning to recognize when it's guiding you and when fear or bias may be clouding your judgment.

2. Differentiate Intuition from Fear

- Intuition often feels calm and certain, even if the decision it suggests is bold. Fear, on the other hand, is usually accompanied by anxiety and a sense of panic.
- **Reflection Prompt**: "Does this feeling stem from confidence and clarity, or is it rooted in fear and self-doubt?"

3. Listen to Your Inner Voice

- Your intuition often speaks quietly, so create space to hear it. This might involve taking a walk, meditating, or journaling about your feelings.
- **Exercise**: When faced with a decision, pause and ask yourself, "What does my gut say?"

4. Trust Patterns from Experience

- Intuition is strongest when it's informed by past experiences. If a situation feels familiar, your intuition might be drawing on lessons you've already learned.
- **Practical Tip**: Reflect on times when you trusted your intuition in the past. What was the outcome, and what can you learn from it?

5. Combine Intuition with Logic

- Intuition and logic aren't mutually exclusive; they work best together. Use intuition to guide you toward a decision and logic to validate or refine it.
- **Example**: If your gut tells you to pursue a job opportunity, research the company and role to confirm it aligns with your goals.

6. Practice Mindfulness to Strengthen Intuition

- Mindfulness helps you stay present and attuned to your internal signals. Regular mindfulness practices can enhance your ability to trust and interpret your intuition.
- **Quick Exercise**: Spend five minutes each day focusing on your breath and observing your thoughts without judgment.

Real-Life Examples of Confident Risk-Taking
1. Elon Musk: Betting It All on Vision

- Elon Musk risked his fortune to fund Tesla and SpaceX, facing the possibility of bankruptcy. His calculated risk, combined with unwavering belief in his vision, paid off, revolutionizing industries.
- **Lesson**: High risk can lead to high reward when combined with careful planning and determination.

2. Sara Blakely: Trusting a Gut Feeling

- Sara Blakely, the founder of Spanx, started her company with $5,000 and no prior experience in fashion. Her intuition told her she was onto something big, and she trusted it despite initial rejections from manufacturers and investors.
- **Lesson**: Intuition, when paired with persistence, can lead to groundbreaking success.

3. Jeff Bezos: Leaving Stability for Opportunity

- Jeff Bezos left a high-paying job to start Amazon, despite the risks of entering an untested e-commerce market. His calculated decision to take this bold step transformed retail forever.
- **Lesson**: Confidence in your calculations and willingness to embrace risk can yield extraordinary results.

Action Steps to Take Risks with Confidence

1. **Conduct a Risk Assessment**
    - Before making a decision, write down:
        - The goal of the risk
        - Potential rewards
        - Possible downsides
        - Mitigation strategies
2. **Engage in Low-Stakes Risk Practice**
    - Build your confidence by taking small risks in everyday life, such as trying a new hobby, speaking up in a meeting, or introducing yourself to a stranger.
3. **Develop a Support System**
    - Surround yourself with people who encourage and support your risk-taking endeavors. Their perspective and advice can boost your confidence.
4. **Track Your Progress**
    - Keep a journal of risks you've taken, outcomes you've achieved, and lessons learned. Reviewing your successes reinforces your belief in your ability to handle challenges.
5. **Visualize Success**
    - Spend time imagining the best possible outcome of the risk you're considering. This mental rehearsal can build excitement and reduce anxiety.

Conclusion: Bold Risks, Bold Rewards

Taking risks with confidence doesn't mean eliminating fear or guaranteeing success. It means being willing to step into uncertainty armed with preparation, self-trust, and the courage to act. By calculating risks and trusting your intuition, you can make bold moves that align with your dreams and values.

As you move forward, remember that every leap of faith, no matter how small, brings you closer to a life of growth, purpose, and fulfillment.

Chapter 5: Living Boldly Every Day

Living boldly isn't about grand, sporadic acts of courage—it's about cultivating a fearless mindset and consistently making bold moves that align with your values and goals. It's about showing up every day with purpose, intention, and the determination to embrace life's challenges and opportunities. In this chapter, we'll explore how to build a fearless mindset and integrate boldness into your daily life to foster continuous growth and fulfillment.

Building a Fearless Mindset

Fearlessness doesn't mean the absence of fear—it means mastering it. A fearless mindset allows you to approach challenges with confidence and resilience, empowering you to live boldly every day. Here's how to develop and strengthen this mindset:

1. Reframe Fear as a Signal for Growth

- Fear often arises when we're stepping outside our comfort zone. Instead of viewing fear as a warning to retreat, reframe it as a signal that you're on the brink of growth.
- **Mantra**: "Fear is the compass that points me toward progress."

2. Practice Self-Awareness

- Understand your triggers, limitations, and emotional responses. Self-awareness helps you identify when fear is holding you back and enables you to respond intentionally rather than react impulsively.
- **Exercise**: Take five minutes each evening to reflect on moments when fear influenced your decisions. What could you do differently next time?

3. Cultivate Resilience

- Fearlessness requires resilience—the ability to bounce back from setbacks and adapt to challenges. Build resilience by focusing on solutions rather than problems and learning from every experience.
- **Reflection Prompt**: "How can I use this setback as a stepping stone to move forward?"

4. Embrace Vulnerability

- Living boldly means being willing to take risks and expose yourself to potential failure or rejection. Vulnerability is not a weakness but a sign of strength and authenticity.
- **Key Insight**: "The willingness to be vulnerable is what makes boldness powerful."

5. Surround Yourself with Bold Influences

- The people around you shape your mindset. Surround yourself with individuals who inspire you to think big, take risks, and pursue your dreams.
- **Practical Tip**: Join groups or communities that encourage bold thinking and action.

6. Focus on Your Inner Dialogue

- Your thoughts shape your reality. Replace self-doubt and negative thinking with affirmations and empowering beliefs.
- **Affirmations for Boldness:**
  - "I am capable of achieving great things."

- ◦ "Challenges are opportunities in disguise."
- ◦ "I am stronger than my fears."

7. Take Ownership of Your Decisions

- Bold living requires accountability. Own your choices, whether they lead to success or failure, and use every outcome as a chance to grow.
- **Mantra**: "I am the architect of my life."

How to Keep Growing Through Bold Moves

Bold living is a continuous journey, not a one-time destination. To keep growing, you must regularly challenge yourself, embrace new opportunities, and push beyond your comfort zone. Here are strategies to ensure boldness remains a part of your daily life:

1. Set Bold Goals

- Bold goals inspire bold action. Set ambitious but achievable targets that stretch your limits and encourage growth.
- **Example**: Instead of aiming to "get better at public speaking," set a goal to "deliver a keynote speech at a major event within a year."

2. Take Daily Bold Actions

- Integrate boldness into your routine by committing to one courageous act each day. This could be as simple as voicing your opinion, trying a new activity, or reaching out to someone you admire.
- **Challenge**: Start a "Bold Action Journal" and record one bold thing you do each day.

3. Embrace Change

- Growth requires change. Be open to new ideas, experiences, and perspectives, even if they feel uncomfortable at first.
- **Reflection Prompt**: "What's one thing I can change today to move closer to my goals?"

4. Seek Feedback and Learn from It

- Feedback is a powerful tool for growth. Ask for constructive input from mentors, peers, or trusted individuals, and use it to refine your approach.

- **Practical Tip**: After completing a bold action, ask, "What went well, and what could I improve next time?"

5. Celebrate Progress, Not Just Success

- Acknowledge and celebrate every step forward, regardless of the outcome. Progress, not perfection, is what matters most.
- **Exercise**: At the end of each week, list three bold actions you took and what you learned from them.

6. Expand Your Comfort Zone

- Continuously push the boundaries of what feels comfortable. Over time, actions that once seemed bold will become second nature.
- **Practical Tip**: Identify one area of your life where you feel stuck and commit to taking a bold step in that direction.

7. Invest in Personal Growth

- Growth requires ongoing learning and development. Read books, attend workshops, and seek experiences that challenge and inspire you.
- **Key Insight**: "Boldness grows when you expose yourself to new knowledge and opportunities."

8. Embrace Failure as Part of the Process

- Failure is inevitable when you're living boldly. Instead of fearing it, view it as proof that you're trying, learning, and growing.
- **Mantra**: "Every failure brings me closer to success."

Real-Life Examples of Bold Living
1. Richard Branson: Embracing Bold Risks

- Richard Branson, founder of Virgin Group, attributes much of his success to bold decision-making. From starting a record company to launching an airline, he has consistently taken risks that align with his passions and vision.
- **Lesson**: Bold living is about pursuing what excites you, even if it feels risky.

2. Malala Yousafzai: Bold Advocacy for Education

- Despite facing threats to her life, Malala Yousafzai boldly advocated for girls' education in her home country of Pakistan. Her courage not only changed her life but inspired a global movement.
- **Lesson**: Boldness can create ripple effects that transform the world.

3. Steve Jobs: Bold Innovation

- Steve Jobs revolutionized technology by consistently thinking outside the box and taking bold risks. His fearless mindset allowed him to turn Apple into one of the most innovative companies in the world.
- **Lesson**: Bold moves often lead to groundbreaking innovation and success.

Practical Exercises for Daily Boldness

1. **The Boldness Challenge**
   - For 30 days, commit to doing one thing each day that scares or challenges you. At the end of the challenge, reflect on how you've grown.
2. **The "Why Not?" Experiment**
   - When faced with an opportunity, instead of defaulting to "no," ask yourself, "Why not?" This mindset encourages you to explore possibilities you might otherwise dismiss.
3. **Visualize Bold Outcomes**
   - Spend five minutes each morning visualizing yourself taking bold actions and achieving your goals. This practice builds confidence and sets a fearless tone for the day.
4. **Create a Bold Role Model Board**
   - Compile images, quotes, and stories of people you admire for their boldness. Use this board as a source of inspiration when you need a confidence boost.

Conclusion: A Life Lived Boldly

Living boldly every day is a choice—a commitment to face challenges with courage, embrace growth, and pursue your dreams fearlessly. By building a fearless mindset and consistently making bold moves, you create a life filled with purpose, excitement, and fulfillment.

As you move forward, remember that bold living is not about perfection but persistence. It's about showing up, trying, and learning from every experience.

Appendix A: Exercises for Developing Daily Courage

Courage is like a muscle—it strengthens with practice and consistent effort. Integrating daily exercises into your routine can help you build the courage needed to face challenges, embrace opportunities, and live boldly. This appendix provides a variety of practical exercises designed to help you cultivate courage incrementally. These activities focus on self-awareness, small acts of bravery, and mindset shifts to foster resilience and fearlessness.

1. The Courage Journal

Purpose: Track and celebrate your courageous actions to build self-confidence.

- **How to Do It:**
  Each evening, write down one courageous act you performed during the day. It could be as simple as speaking up in a meeting, trying a new activity, or saying "no" to something that didn't serve you.
    - Include:
        - What you did.
        - How you felt before, during, and after.
        - What you learned from the experience.
    - Over time, review your journal to recognize your growth and identify patterns in your courageous behavior.

2. The 5-Minute Fear Challenge

Purpose: Practice confronting fear in manageable, short bursts.

- **How to Do It:**
  Dedicate five minutes daily to facing something you've been avoiding because of fear. Examples include:
    - Sending an email you've been procrastinating on.
    - Initiating a difficult conversation.
    - Trying a skill or activity you feel uncertain about.
    - The short time frame makes the task less intimidating, and regular practice desensitizes you to fear.

3. The Mirror of Courage

Purpose: Build self-awareness and self-affirmation.

- **How to Do It:**
    - Stand in front of a mirror for two minutes each morning and speak affirmations aloud. Examples include:
        - "I am braver than my fears."
        - "I have the strength to face any challenge today."
        - "Every small act of courage makes me stronger."
    - Look yourself in the eye as you say these affirmations to internalize their meaning and build self-belief.

4. The Gratitude-Courage Connection

Purpose: Use gratitude to reframe fear and build courage.

- **How to Do It:**
  - At the end of each day, write down one fear you faced and something you're grateful for because of it. For example:
    - "I'm grateful I spoke up during the meeting because it showed my boss I have valuable ideas."
  - This exercise helps you see fear as a stepping stone to positive outcomes and reinforces the habit of acting courageously.

5. Micro-Risks for Macro-Gains

Purpose: Strengthen your courage muscle by taking small, low-stakes risks.

- **How to Do It:**
  - Each day, identify one micro-risk you can take. Examples:
    - Try a new food.
    - Talk to someone you don't usually interact with.
    - Volunteer to take on a new responsibility at work.
  - Over time, these small risks build your confidence for larger challenges.

6. Visualization for Courage

Purpose: Mentally rehearse successful outcomes to reduce fear and boost confidence.

- **How to Do It:**
  - Spend five minutes each morning visualizing yourself successfully completing a challenging or intimidating task.
  - Picture every detail: your actions, your emotions, and the positive outcome.
  - Regular visualization strengthens your belief in your ability to handle difficult situations.

7. The Courage Buddy System

Purpose: Gain accountability and encouragement by sharing your goals with someone you trust.

- **How to Do It:**
  - Partner with a friend, mentor, or coworker who also wants to build courage.
  - Share one courageous action you plan to take each day and check in with each other for encouragement and accountability.
  - Celebrate each other's successes and provide support during setbacks.

8. Fear Exposure Ladder

Purpose: Gradually confront fears in a structured way.

- **How to Do It:**
    - Write down a fear you want to overcome (e.g., public speaking).
    - Break it down into smaller steps, ranked from least to most intimidating. For example:
        - Step 1: Speak in front of a mirror.
        - Step 2: Share an idea during a small group meeting.
        - Step 3: Deliver a short presentation to a supportive audience.
        - Step 4: Speak at a larger event.
    - Tackle one step at a time, celebrating your progress as you go.

9. Courage Anchors

Purpose: Use physical objects or rituals to remind yourself of your bravery.

- **How to Do It:**
    - Choose an object (e.g., a bracelet, coin, or small stone) that symbolizes courage for you.
    - Carry it with you and touch it whenever you feel fear, reminding yourself of your past courageous actions.
    - Alternatively, create a ritual, such as taking three deep breaths or repeating a mantra, to anchor yourself in bravery.

10. The Weekly Boldness Audit

Purpose: Reflect on your progress and set goals for continued growth.

- **How to Do It:**
  - At the end of each week, ask yourself:
    - What bold actions did I take this week?
    - What fears did I confront?
    - What did I learn from these experiences?
    - What bold move can I plan for next week?
  - Use your answers to set intentional goals and celebrate your achievements.

11. The "Why Not?" Exercise

Purpose: Encourage openness to opportunities by shifting your mindset.

- **How to Do It:**
  - When faced with a decision, instead of defaulting to "no" out of fear, ask yourself, "Why not?"
  - Evaluate the potential rewards versus the risks and commit to saying "yes" to one opportunity each day that excites or challenges you.

12. The Morning Courage Ritual

Purpose: Start each day with a bold mindset.

- **How to Do It:**
  - Dedicate five minutes each morning to a ritual that boosts your courage. This might include:
    - Reviewing your goals.
    - Practicing gratitude.
    - Repeating affirmations.
    - Visualizing success.
  - This practice sets a fearless tone for the day ahead.

13. The Courage Role Model Reflection

Purpose: Learn from the examples of others.

- **How to Do It:**
  - Identify someone you admire for their courage (e.g., a historical figure, mentor, or friend).
  - Reflect on their bold actions and ask yourself:
    - What qualities made them courageous?
    - How can I emulate those qualities in my own life?
  - Write down one lesson from their story and how you'll apply it.

Conclusion: The Daily Practice of Courage

Courage is not a one-time act but a daily practice. By incorporating these exercises into your routine, you'll develop the confidence, resilience, and boldness needed to face challenges, embrace opportunities, and live authentically. Remember, every small act of courage contributes to your growth, and over time, these small steps lead to monumental transformations. Keep practicing, keep growing, and keep living boldly.

Message from the Author:

I hope you enjoyed this book, I love astrology and knew there was not a book such as this out on the shelf. I love metaphysical items as well. Please check out my other books:

-Life of Government Benefits

-My life of Hell

-My life with Hydrocephalus

-Red Sky

-World Domination:Woman's rule

-World Domination:Woman's Rule 2: The War

-Life and Banishment of Apophis: book 1

-The Kidney Friendly Diet

-The Ultimate Hemp Cookbook

-Creating a Dispensary(legally)

-Cleanliness throughout life: the importance of showering from childhood to adulthood.

-Strong Roots: The Risks of Overcoddling children

-Hemp Horoscopes: Cosmic Insights and Earthly Healing

- Celestial Hemp Navigating the Zodiac: Through the Green Cosmos

-Astrological Hemp: Aligning The Stars with Earth's Ancient Herb

-The Astrological Guide to Hemp: Stars, Signs, and Sacred Leaves

-Green Growth: Innovative Marketing Strategies for your Hemp Products and Dispensary

-Cosmic Cannabis

-Astrological Munchies

-Henry The Hemp

-Zodiacal Roots: The Astrological Soul Of Hemp

- Green Constellations: Intersection of Hemp and Zodiac

-Hemp in The Houses: An astrological Adventure Through The Cannabis Galaxy

-Galactic Ganja Guide

Heavenly Hemp

Zodiac Leaves

Doctor Who Astrology

Cannastrology

Stellar Satvias and Cosmic Indicas

<u>Celestial Cannabis: A Zodiac Journey</u>

AstroHerbology: The Sky and The Soil: Volume 1

AstroHerbology:Celestial Cannabis:Volume 2

Cosmic Cannabis Cultivation

The Starry Guide to Herbal Harmony: Volume 1

The Starry Guide to Herbal Harmony: Cannabis Universe: Volume 2

Yugioh Astrology: Astrological Guide to Deck, Duels and more

Nightmare Mansion: Echoes of The Abyss

Nightmare Mansion 2: Legacy of Shadows

Nightmare Mansion 3: Shadows of the Forgotten

Nightmare Mansion 4: Echoes of the Damned

The Life and Banishment of Apophis: Book 2

Nightmare Mansion: Halls of Despair

<u>Healing with Herb: Cannabis and Hydrocephalus</u>

<u>Planetary Pot: Aligning with Astrological Herbs: Volume 1</u>

Fast Track to Freedom: 30 Days to Financial Independence Using AI, Assets, and Agile Hustles

<u>Cosmic Hemp Pathways</u>

How to Become Financially Free in 30 Days: 10,000 Paths to Prosperity

Zodiacal Herbage: Astrological Insights: Volume 1

Nightmare Mansion: Whispers in the Walls

The Daleks Invade Atlantis
Henry the hemp and Hydrocephalus

10X The Kidney Friendly Diet
Cannabis Universe: Adult coloring book
Hemp Astrology: The Healing Power of the Stars
Zodiacal Herbage: Astrological Insights: Cannabis Universe: Volume 2
<u>Planetary Pot: Aligning with Astrological Herbs: Cannabis Universes: Volume 2</u>
Doctor Who Meets the Replicators and SG-1: The Ultimate Battle for Survival
Nightmare Mansion: Curse of the Blood Moon
<u>The Celestial Stoner: A Guide to the Zodiac</u>
Cosmic Pleasures: Sex Toy Astrology for Every Sign
Hydrocephalus Astrology: Navigating the Stars and Healing Waters
Lapis and the Mischievous Chocolate Bar

Celestial Positions: Sexual Astrology for Every Sign
Apophis's Shadow Work Journal: : A Journey of Self-Discovery and Healing
Kinky Cosmos: Sexual Kink Astrology for Every Sign
Digital Cosmos: The Astrological Digimon Compendium
Stellar Seeds: The Cosmic Guide to Growing with Astrology
Apophis's Daily Gratitude Journal

Cat Astrology: Feline Mysteries of the Cosmos
The Cosmic Kama Sutra: An Astrological Guide to Sexual Positions
Unleash Your Potential: A Guided Journal Powered by AI Insights
Whispers of the Enchanted Grove

Cosmic Pleasures: An Astrological Guide to Sexual Kinks

369, 12 Manifestation Journal

Whisper of the nocturne journal(blank journal for writing or drawing)

The Boogey Book

Locked In Reflection: A Chastity Journey Through Locktober

Generating Wealth Quickly:

How to Generate $100,000 in 24 Hours

Star Magic: Harness the Power of the Universe

The Flatulence Chronicles: A Fart Journal for Self-Discovery

The Doctor and The Death Moth

Seize the Day: A Personal Seizure Tracking Journal

The Ultimate Boogeyman Safari: A Journey into the Boogie World and Beyond

Whispers of Samhain: 1,000 Spells of Love, Luck, and Lunar Magic: Samhain Spell Book

Apophis's guides:

Witch's Spellbook Crafting Guide for Halloween

<u>Frost & Flame: The Enchanted Yule Grimoire of 1000 Winter Spells</u>

<u>The Ultimate Boogey Goo Guide & Spooky Activities for Halloween Fun</u>

Harmony of the Scales: A Libra's Spellcraft for Balance and Beauty

The Enchanted Advent: 36 Days of Christmas Wonders

Nightmare Mansion: The Labyrinth of Screams

Harvest of Enchantment: 1,000 Spells of Gratitude, Love, and Fortune for Thanksgiving

The Boogey Chronicles: A Journal of Nightly Encounters and Shadowy Secrets

The 12 Days of Financial Freedom: A Step-by-Step Christmas Countdown to Transform Your Finances

Sigil of the Eternal Spiral Blank Journal

A Christmas Feast: Timeless Recipes for Every Meal

Holiday Stress-Free Solutions: A Survival Guide to Thriving During the Festive Season

Yu-Gi-Oh! Holiday Gifting Mastery: The Ultimate Guide for Fans and Newcomers Alike

Holiday Harmony: A Hydrocephalus Survival Guide for the Festive Season

Celestial Craft: The Witch's Almanac for 2025 – A Cosmic Guide to Manifestations, Moons, and Mystical Events

Doctor Who: The Toymaker's Winter Wonderland

Tulsa King Unveiled: A Thrilling Guide to Stallone's Mafia Masterpiece

Pendulum Craft: A Complete Guide to Crafting and Using Personalized Divination Tools

Nightmare Mansion: Santa's Eternal Eve

Starlight Noel: A Cosmic Journey through Christmas Mysteries

The Dark Architect: Unlocking the Blueprint of Existence

Surviving the Embrace: The Ultimate Guide to Encounters with The Hugging Molly

The Enchanted Codex: Secrets of the Craft for Witches, Wiccans, and Pagans

Harvest of Gratitude: A Complete Thanksgiving Guide

Yuletide Essentials: A Complete Guide to an Authentic and Magical Christmas

Celestial Smokes: A Cosmic Guide to Cigars and Astrology

Living in Balance: A Comprehensive Survival Guide to Thriving with Diabetes Insipidus

Cosmic Symbiosis: The Venom Zodiac Chronicles

The Cursed Paw of Ambition

Cosmic Symbiosis: The Astrological Venom Journal

Celestial Wonders Unfold: A Stargazer's Guide to the Cosmos (2024-2029)

The Ultimate Black Friday Prepper's Guide: Mastering Shopping Strategies and Savings

Cosmic Sales: The Astrological Guide to Black Friday Shopping

Legends of the Corn Mother and Other Harvest Myths

Whispers of the Harvest: The Corn Mother's Journal

The Evergreen Spellbook

The Doctor Meets the Boogeyman

The White Witch of Rose Hall's SpellBook

The Gingerbread Golem's Shadow: A Study in Sweet Darkness

The Gingerbread Golem Codex: An Academic Exploration of Sweet Myths

The Gingerbread Golem Grimoire: Sweet Magicks and Spells for the Festive Witch

The Curse of the Gingerbread Golem

10-minute Christmas Crafts for kids

<u>Christmas Crisis Solutions: The Ultimate Last-Minute Survival Guide</u>

Gingerbread Golem Recipes: Holiday Treats with a Magical Twist

The Infinite Key: Unlocking Mystical Secrets of the Ages

Enchanted Yule: A Wiccan and Pagan Guide to a Magical and Memorable Season

Dinosaurs of Power: Unlocking Ancient Magick

Astro-Dinos: The Cosmic Guide to Prehistoric Wisdom

Gallifrey's Yule Logs: A Festive Doctor Who Cookbook

The Dino Grimoire: Secrets of Prehistoric Magick

The Gift They Never Knew They Needed

The Gingerbread Golem's Culinary Alchemy: Enchanting Recipes for a Sweetly Dark Feast

A Time Lord Christmas: Holiday Adventures with the Doctor

Krampusproofing Your Home: Defensive Strategies for Yule

Silent Frights: A Collection of Christmas Creepypastas to Chill Your Bones

Santa Raptor's Jolly Carnage: A Dino-Claus Christmas Tale

Prehistoric Palettes: A Dino Wicca Coloring Journey
The Christmas Wishkeeper Chronicles
The Starlight Sleigh: A Holiday Journey
Elf Secrets: The True Magic of the North Pole
Candy Cane Conjurations
Cooking with Kids: Recipes Under 20 Minutes
Doctor Who: The TARDIS Confiscation
The Anxiety First Aid Kit: Quick Tools to Calm Your Mind
Frosty Whispers: A Winter's Tale
The Infinite Key: Unlocking the Secrets to Prosperity, Resilience, and Purpose
The Grasping Void: Why You'll Regret This Purchase
Astrology for Busy Bees: Star Signs Simplified
The Instant Focus Formula: Cut Through the Noise
The Secret Language of Colors: Unlocking the Emotional Codes
Sacred Fossil Chronicles: Blank Journal
The Christmas Cottage Miracle
Feeding Frenzy: Graboid-Inspired Recipes
Manifest in Minutes: The Quick Law of Attraction Guide
The Symbiote Chronicles: Doctor Who's Venomous Journey
Think Tiny, Grow Big: The Minimalist Mindset
The Energy Key: Unlocking Limitless Motivation
New Year, New Magic: Manifesting Your Best Year Yet
Unstoppable You: Mastering Confidence in Minutes
Infinite Energy: The Secret to Never Feeling Drained
Lightning Focus: Mastering the Art of Productivity in a Distracted World
Saturnalia Manifestation Magick: A Guide to Unlocking Abundance During the Solstice
Graboids and Garland: The Ultimate Tremors-Themed Christmas Guide
12 Nights of Holiday Magic
The Power of Pause: 60-Second Mindfulness Practices

The Quick Reset: How to Reclaim Your Life After Burnout

The Shadow Eater: A Tale of Despair and Survival

The Micro-Mastery Method: Transform Your Skills in Just Minutes a Day

Reclaiming Time: How to Live More by Doing Less

Chronovore: The Eternal Nexus

The Mind Reset: Unlocking Your Inner Peace in a Chaotic World

Confidence Code: Building Unshakable Self-Belief

Baby the Vampire Terrier

Baby the Vampire Terrier's Christmas Adventure

Celestial Streams: The Content Creator's Astrology Manual

The Wealth Whisperer: Unlocking Abundance with Everyday Actions

The Energy Equation: Maximize Your Output Without Burning Out

The Happiness Algorithm: Science-Backed Steps to Joyful Living

Stress-Free Success: Achieving Goals Without Anxiety

Mindful Wealth: The New Blueprint for Financial Freedom

The Festive Flavors of New Year: A Culinary Celebration

The Master's Gambit: Keys of Eternal Power

Shadowed Secrets: Groundhog Day Mysteries

Beneath the Burrow: Lessons from the Groundhog

Spring's Whispers: The Groundhog's Prediction

The Limitless Mindset: Unlock Your Untapped Potential

The Focus Funnel: How to Cut Through Chaos and Get Results

If you want solar for your home go here: https://www.harborso-
lar.live/apophisenterprises/

Get Some Tarot cards: https://www.makeplayingcards.com/sell/apophis-occult-shop

Get some shirts: https://www.bonfire.com/store/apophis-shirt-emporium/

<u>Instagrams:</u>
@apophis_enterprises,
@apophisbookemporium,
@apophisscardshop
Twitter: @apophisenterpr1
 Tiktok:@apophisenterprise
Youtube: @sg1fan23477, @FiresideRetreatKingdom
Hive: @sg1fan23477
CheeLee: @SG1fan23477

  –

Podcast: Apophis Chat Zone: https://open.spotify.com/show/5zXbrCLEV2xzCp8ybrfHsk?si=fb4d4fdbdce44dec

Newsletter: https://apophiss-newsletter-27c897.beehiiv.com/

If you want to support me or see posts of other projects that I have come over to: **buymeacoffee.com/mpetchinskg**
I post there daily several times a day

Get your Dinowicca or Christmas themed digital products, especially Santa Raptor songs and other musics. Here:
https://sg1fan23477.gumroad.com

Apophis Yuletide Digital has not only digital Christmas items, but it will have all things with Dinowicca as well as other Digital products.